Earth Basics

Rocks

by Rebecca Pettiford

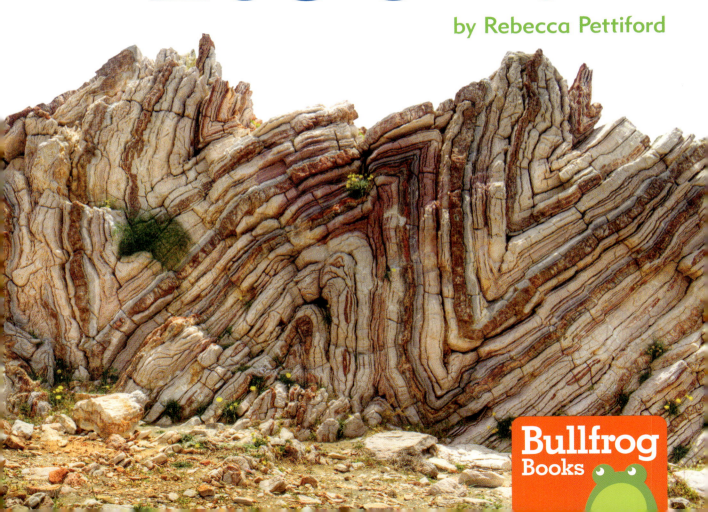

Bullfrog Books

Ideas for Parents and Teachers

Bullfrog Books let children practice reading informational text at the earliest reading levels. Repetition, familiar words, and photo labels support early readers.

Before Reading
- Discuss the cover photo. What does it tell them?
- Look at the picture glossary together. Read and discuss the words.

Read the Book
- "Walk" through the book and look at the photos. Let the child ask questions. Point out the photo labels.
- Read the book to the child, or have him or her read independently.

After Reading
- Prompt the child to think more. Ask: Rocks are used to make many things in homes and buildings. Have you seen something built out of rocks? What was it?

Bullfrog Books are published by Jump!
5357 Penn Avenue South
Minneapolis, MN 55419
www.jumplibrary.com

Copyright © 2024 Jump! International copyright reserved in all countries. No part of this book may be reproduced in any form without written permission from the publisher.

Library of Congress Cataloging-in-Publication Data is available at www.loc.gov or upon request from the publisher.

ISBN: 979-8-88524-442-8 (hardcover)
ISBN: 979-8-88524-443-5 (paperback)
ISBN: 979-8-88524-444-2 (ebook)

Editor: Katie Chanez
Designer: Emma Almgren-Bersie

Photo Credits: cherezoff/Shutterstock, cover; Matauw/Shutterstock, 1; PTZ Pictures/Shutterstock, 3; iacomino FRiMAGES/Shutterstock, 4; Photosampler/Shutterstock, 5, 23bm; Clarity Photography/Shutterstock, 6–7 (top); www.sandatlas.org/Shutterstock, 6–7 (right), 15, 23bl; Pics Man24/Shutterstock, 6–7 (bottom); Helen Hotson/Shutterstock, 8–9; Hannest/Dreamstime, 10; John D Sirlin/Shutterstock, 11; Fyletto/iStock, 12–13, 23tr; Fotos593/Shutterstock, 16, 23tm; Raul Bal/Shutterstock, 17, 23tl; Artazum/Shutterstock, 18–19 (top); Orhan Cam/Shutterstock, 18–19 (bottom); AnnaStills/Shutterstock, 20–21; VallaV/Shutterstock, 22 (top); michal812/Shutterstock, 22ml; Yes058 Montree Nanta/Shutterstock, 22mr; Susan Newcomb/Shutterstock, 22bl, 23br; xpixel/Shutterstock, 22br; JIANG HONGYAN/Shutterstock, 24.

Printed in the United States of America at Corporate Graphics in North Mankato, Minnesota.

Table of Contents

Three Kinds	4
The Rock Cycle	22
Picture Glossary	23
Index	24
To Learn More	24

Three Kinds

Rocks form on Earth.
They are in the ground.

Minerals make up rocks.

There are three kinds.

Rocks change.

How?

They break up.

It takes a long time.

Water moves rocks.

Wind does, too.

Rocks build up.
Sedimentary rock forms.
See the layers?
Cool!

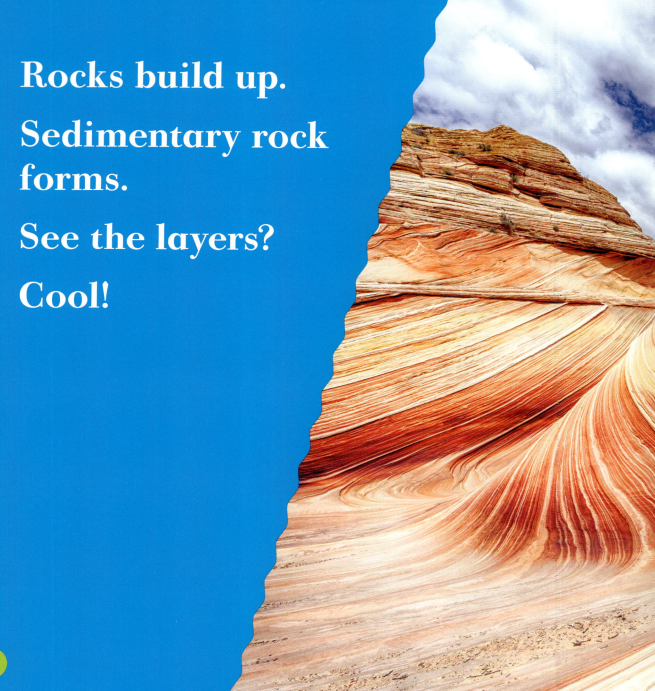

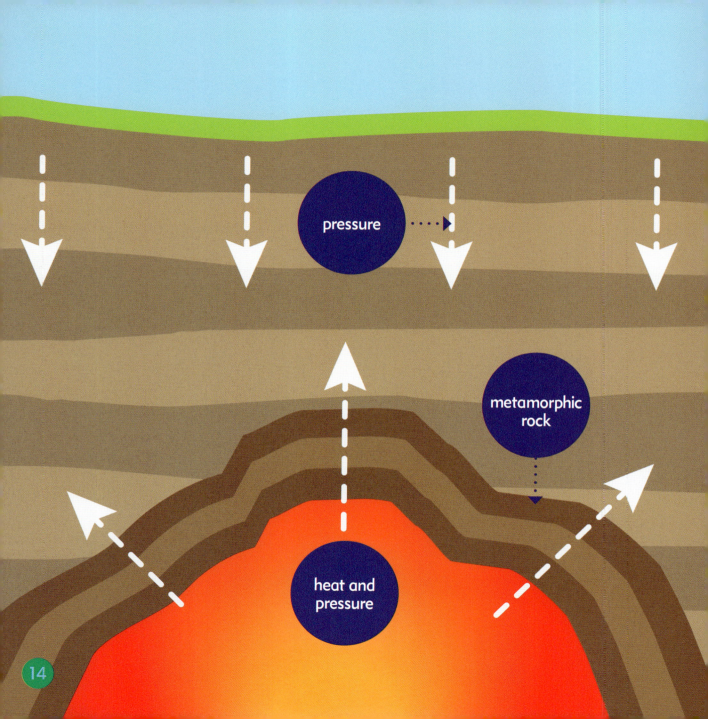

It is hot inside Earth.
The ground is heavy.
It pushes down.
Rock changes.
Now it is metamorphic.

metamorphic rock

Lava comes out.
It is hot.

It cools.

It makes igneous rock.

igneous rock

granite

marble

We build with rocks.

Rocks are all around!
Where do you see them?

The Rock Cycle

Rocks are always changing. Take a look at the rock cycle!

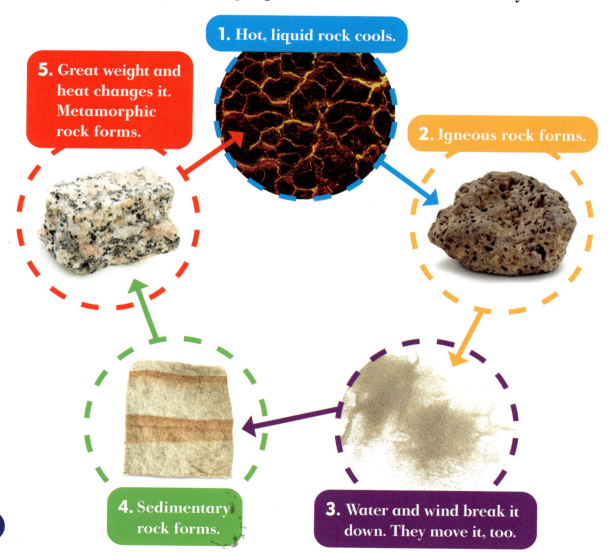

Picture Glossary

igneous rock
Rock that forms when hot, liquid rock cools.

lava
Hot, liquid rock that comes from inside Earth.

layers
Parts of something that lie over or under other parts.

metamorphic rock
Rock that forms when other rocks are put under great pressure or heat.

minerals
Hard substances found on Earth that do not come from animals or plants.

sedimentary rock
Rock that forms from bits of rock, plants, and animals.

Index

build 12, 19
change 9, 15
Earth 4, 15
ground 4, 15
igneous rock 17
lava 16
layers 12
metamorphic rock 15
minerals 5
sedimentary rock 12
water 10
wind 11

To Learn More

Finding more information is as easy as 1, 2, 3.
① Go to www.factsurfer.com
② Enter "rocks" into the search box.
③ Choose your book to see a list of websites.